Broken But Still Standing

By

Paulette Nelson

Unless otherwise noted, all Scripture quotations are from The Holy Bible, King James Version (KJV)

Library of Congress
Cataloging-in-Publication Data
        Nelson, Paulette
        Religion: Inspirational

Library of Congress Control Number:
        2012933054

ISBN: 978-0-9849360-3-8

Edited by: Michelle A. Nelson
                    Candice M. Nelson
Photos by: Thaddeus Tatum
Cover Design: Brittany J. Jackson
Published by G Publishing, LLC

Printed in the United States of America

DEDICATION

First and foremost, to God through Him I can do all things.

> *"In all things we are more than conquerors..."* Romans 8:37

My father who was always there for me.

My Mother whose strength is amazing.

> *"Honor your father and mother..."* Ephesians 6:2

My children and my grandchildren who have my heart, and have given me so much support.

All my children who call me Mom who have inspired me.

"Train up a child in the way it should go an it shall not depart..." Proverbs 22:6

My sister & brother and all my family & friends who show me so much love. Special Thanks to Thaddeus for all your help.

"...Love never fails"
1Corinthians 13:4-8

ACKNOWLEDGMENTS

I thank GOD for the opportunity that he has given me. My hope for this book is that it will lift someone spirits and be an inspiration. In addition, that it will help someone who may be going through to realize that they are not along. *"Comfort each other & edify one another."* 1 Peter 4:7-11

I have been trying to express the words that are in this book for many years. I realize that this is my season. *"A time to weep, and a time to laugh, a time to mourn, and a time to dance."* Ecclesiastes 3:1-8

May God continue to bless you. May you grow closer to him is my prayer. A special thanks to all that have helped me in one way or another.

TABLE OF CONTENTS

INTRODUCTION

"The things which are seen are temporal; but the things which are not seen are eternal." 2CO 4:18

When reading this book you will find times where my faith in God brought me through the storms & into the light. *"Therefore, having been justified by faith, we have peace with God through our Lord Jesus Christ."* Romans 5:1

Starting from an early age in my life, I found Jesus. *"We are his workmanship created in Christ Jesus for good works."* Ephesians 2:10

My parents raised me & my siblings in church, sometimes four times a week. Therefore, they gave me great foundation a rock in which to stand on.

Within this book, I will touch on issues such as leaving home, marriage, raising children, losing a love one, caring for parents and more. All will be discussed in detail.

So here we go. BE BLESSED.

Paulette Nelson

CHAPTER 1: Connections

Well this is a story of a woman *Broken But Still Standing* started a long time ago. I can recall being so young, always wanting to please people; wanting to love and be loved. I trusted in God, I had a typical family mom, dad, one brother and a sister. Then I grew up, wow I actually grew up. I went away to college. I was not happy about being away from my mom and dad and staying on campus. I did not really have a college life, met some people and saw things that I did not normally see. I had a strict childhood, my mom kept us pretty sheltered, but she loved her children. My dad was a wonderful father; he would come and pick me up on the weekends, which was an hour away from home, even though he was tired from work. I never really appreciated what my father did, until I began to work. Being tired and just wanting to go home, kick off my shoes, and relax. My dad never did that; he wanted to pick me up first, ensuring I was home with my family, having a relaxing weekend.

Let me take you back to when I fell in love. I was in high school and he was a football player. I dated a few people, when I met him, the love he showed me made me sure he was the one for me. There was no doubt in my mind that he loved me; he just showed me the only way he knew how. Which I later learned that it was not the way I wanted to be loved. He had come from what appeared to be a broken home. A large family with many issues that was present in his life at the time. There were things that were going on that I found out later on in the relationship that people tried to tell me about, but I just chose to look pass it.   I was eighteen years old going to college, he had not graduated yet from high school, but he was the one in my eyes.   The first time I was intimate with a person, it was with him, and ended up getting pregnant and having my first child at the age of nineteen. He was a usual young man of my times, not wanting to be tied down with a pregnant woman. He of course, was not ready to get married, so I had many days of crying ahead. My friends were supportive, taking me out to make me feel better.

We had a beautiful baby girl, three months before her delivery, my doctor discovered that I had fibroids and placed me on bed rest to ensure the survival of my daughter and myself. With that came the ultimate sacrifice, I had to drop out of college and prepare myself for the journey we call parenthood up ahead. It was so good to know that with God all things are possible. I managed to be the best mother I could through prayer and faith in God. I was encouraged by my parents and friends, but it was not hard for me to believe and I knew that God would strengthen me and that is what I leaned on.

I remember when my first-born was just a little baby, and wow, things seemed so overwhelming. Me being distraught, from not seeing her father, and the lack of love from him in the way I thought I should be, I became overwhelmed. I remember going to my room upstairs, in my parents' house, and I was looking out of the window in the front of the house. I can recall thinking that, "this fall would be pretty hard if I jumped out of this window." I knew that I would not have survived the fall and I still wanted to jump. This

Paulette Nelson

was the only time in my life, and believe me I've had some rough times since then, but that was the only time that the devil sort of had taken a hold of me, and I was going to jump. God saw fit to have my daughter cry; and when she cried it snapped me out of it just in time. I thank God because it just wasn't for me, you know you have to endure and hang in there with God because He didn't say it was going to be easy, he didn't say any of those things. He said, "If you just trust in him, lean on him that he would be your strength," and he was my strength since that day. My first-born is thirty-six year old now, so I know that incident was at least thirty-five years ago that I thought about ending my life. You will see along with my story that there has been many of times that I could have ended my life, but I never thought about it again only through the grace of God, I was able to be *Broken But Still Standing*.

Therefore, we went on, she grew up, still at my parents' house, I am working at the hospital and just going through some different times, her dad worked there. Just dealing with women, "Women" we are some funny creatures. We do things to hurt each other; it is so amazing that we can do things like that to each other. There were some treacherous women at our job, they found out that we had a child together and were thinking about getting married. They would bring things back to me, "Oh he's doing this, with this one and…," just brought all the evil and negative thoughts back to me and I fed into them. I am young and not trusting, and when I fed into them it brought so much heartache into my life at the time, but then again, you know I quite the job there. I began telling my mom, "I just needed to get away from there" and she told me, "Well bay I'm going to tell you, that this will probably be the only time in

Paulette Nelson

your life where you can quite a job. The only reason I say this is because you are home with me, but you are going to have to take some things, pray a lot, and just keep going. You can't quite because something goes wrong."

That was the number one lesson that my mother taught me, she let me quit, and she never, never was wrong in making me understand the lesson she was trying to teach me. Believe me I never thought about it, what my mother was saying was so true. You have responsibility when you have a child; it is not about you anymore it is about that child. Therefore, I had to work at jobs I really did not particularly care to much about and we went on. Life was not always bad, I learned another lesson, that people will disappoint you, but God will not disappoint you. If you put your trust in man, you will be disappointed. Therefore, I learned that lesson and I learned how to lean and depend on God more, and he got me through that crisis. I mean sure, there were many other crisis' since, but those were my younger days.

Eventually, when my daughter was five years old, after many trials and different relationships, well not many relationships, but I had a child, I was still at home with my parents and I just wanted to be around them. My life was built around my mom, dad, and daughter. I remember my mom saying, "Well you're lonely, no one's going to come to your door and knock on it and say, 'hey would you like to go out with me?', you know you have to get out there baby..." and she told me those kind of things, my mother is a very wise woman.

I found a good job at another hospital and was doing well and then my child's father asked me to marry him! He came to the job, it was in February of 1980 and proposed to me at the hospital, and it was so exciting! We ended up getting married and had a beautiful big wedding, it was not very expensive my family kicked in and we all bought food together. My fiancé to be just insisted on all his friends being in the wedding, me being shy and quiet I did not have that many friends. Our wedding party ended up being 24 people, I had to go around and ask neighbors and other women I knew to stand up with me, and it turned out to be a very beautiful wedding. Our colors were blue and white, my daughter was the flower girl and it was just very nice. I was now a wife and a mother, and so I had to move on and start my family now!

CHAPTER 2: Growing Up, Married and Moving

We were married on August 23, 1980 and moved into our first place, which was a flat on the west side of town. My husband stayed at home most of the time and I can recall telling my mother, "Wow he never leaves the house" and she would tell me, "Baby don't worry because there will come a time when you wish you knew where he was," and that was not a lie. We ended having another beautiful baby girl in 1981 born in the month of February. Things were still okay for us at the time, I was back to work, and things began to change a little bit around this time. My husband was hanging out with his friends more often, doing some different things that kept him away from the house and I was always concerned. We began to look for a home to purchase for our family, we had a car and we were doing pretty well for a young working couple with children. God was always in my life, but my husband was not a man of the church, meaning he did not attend church. He provided for us, when I did attend church he would always help me get the children ready for service and have dinner ready for us once we made it home.

A couple of years after my second child I experienced a miscarriage, and then in 1983 I had my third child another beautiful baby girl born in July. By this time, we had found a nice ranch style home that we moved into shortly after she was born. I can remember bringing my newborn into the home for the first time. When it was time for him to celebrate his birthday, it always was a special occasion. He believed that he had to party the entire week. I had just had the baby and he wanted a party for his birthday, which was in July. Therefore, we had the party and I was with the new baby, and things were still okay.

I later had another miscarriage before my fourth and final child was born and it was devastating at the time but we got through it. God gave me the strength to get through it and I did, I was back to work but with my fourth child, I was sick during the pregnancy. I was off work most of the time due to being in and out of the hospital about eight times trying to keep my blood pressure and blood sugar down, and I guess it took a toll on my husband. The checks were not coming home anymore; he was under a lot of stress, just getting into lots of situations where he was no longer around the home.

By September of 1986 when my fourth child, my son was born, things had started to get bad. Things went from the bad to worst and so finally, I believed that if I asked for a divorce that he would change. I always hoped that maybe it would snap him out of the things he had started getting himself into, but it did not. I had to muster up all of my strength that I had left to get him out of the house. Our divorced was finalized in 1989 and my son was about three at the time, *Broken, But Still Standing.*

An Author's Note:

I want to take a moment and talk to women for a minute about marrying a person that you are unevenly yoked. I remember thinking when I was younger, mom never told us about being evenly yoked. I am not saying that it is my mother's fault because you have to trust God and ask him for the things that we need. When you go and you step out of his will, you get into things that keep you confused and hurt, you are living a dangerous life. I loved my husband very much, but once I realized that we were unevenly yoked it tore me apart. So if you are going to be in the world, then you marry in the world, but if you want to be in the church then you wait on the Lord. Ask him for what you need and he will provide it for you, don't rush him, don't lead your own way, because if you marry in the church, sure things are not going to be easy just because you are both Christians, but it will be within God's will. Women please remember that you have to do God's will and not your will, ask him for his will and not your will. Remember you may be Broken, But Still Standing!

CHAPTER 3: Single Parenthood - The Children

Now the divorce is final, I have four children and my ex-husband had already lost his job by this time so there was no support coming in from him at all. With the help of my parents, I started to form my role as a single mother to four children. I remained in the home that we were raising our children in taking on a mortgage, utilities, tuition, food, gas, and all necessities of life. My parents would help taking the children back and forth to school while I was working. I later moved them to schools in the area of my job so I could drop them off and pick them up from school.

Growing up we were always raised to believe, The Bible teaches us that without a vision the people will perish. Every year my four children and me would set a goal, we had an old smoking car that would stop on us and smoke up the area so bad that it was driven for work and school only. We could not even go to the drive-thru at a restaurant because the smoke was that bad. My children and I set the goal for that year, that we would get a van that was big enough for everybody. I got my first van from a used car lot in 1990, and the children were excited. During their time in grade school, my children attended private schools; my two younger children were having difficulty learn-ing, so I transferred them to another school. The tuition was very high, but I wanted my children to have a good start to their education. When I was growing up I did not have that chance

Paulette Nelson

or experience, I was very unprepared when I made it to college due to the lack of teaching I received when I was attending grade school. If it were not for my Dad helping me with the term papers and the topic sentences, I would not have made it that far. My English teacher utilized Scope magazines in the 12th grade, we did not have any preparation for college and I did not want that for my children. I wanted them to be prepared so that if they did choose to go to college they would be well equipped for what was in store for them once they made it there.

I watched them grow up through the divorce phase and it made us close. My oldest daughter, she was affected the most by it because she was old enough to understand what was happening and she saw a lot of things when me and their father were going through the divorce. After my divorce, I could not afford to send them to the private schools anymore but my oldest felt as if she would just die if I sent her to a public school for high school. She became so paranoid and scared so I worked harder so she can attend a private high school. The other three attended charter schools, which was still a little bit better than public schools at that time because they did not have large classrooms and more one on one with the students.

For two years after my divorce no one was in life but my children, there was no dating and I worked two jobs most of the time. My oldest went away to college and met some wonderful people that helped me. She was a very smart young woman, 4.0 student, and had won a scholarship that covered her cost for tuition during her first year of school. All of my girls ended up doing very well, they all went away to college, I would pay for the first year and after that, they worked their way through school. My oldest graduated with her Masters and the other two girls received their

Paulette Nelson

Bachelors and are now working towards their Associates in Nursing.

My son had a little bit more difficulty in school, he was diagnosed at an early age with ADHD, which was Attention Deficit Hypertension Disorder, and it was difficult for him to focus. *(Author's Note: To help other parents I am going to make that another chapter in itself.)* As my children were growing up every-body was responsible for chores, I would write their names and chores next to them on the big desk calendar hung on the wall in the kitchen. Everybody would take a week, someone would have the bathroom, kitchen, living room and so on, and we would all work together as a wonderful team. We would have monthly meetings or meetings in between when things began to get chaotic or the devil was intruding on my family. These meetings were respectful meeting, the children were able to speak and talk to me about the things that were going on or about issues that may have been unfair to them. These meetings helped me a lot as a single parent, us working together and keeping them in Sunday school, choir, and all the activities that I felt were good to know and learn the Lord. I felt that it was very important for my children to know the Lord for themselves. My parents helped a lot in raising the children; both my mom and my dad picked them up when they were not working. The children bonded together and helped me stay focused and we all stayed focused.

Things changed as the children got older, as teenagers within the growing process. We were a wonderful family, in fact, my family and friends would be envious of the relationship I had and have with my children. People were always trying to come in between that, but I give God all the Glory because I may be *Broken but I am Still Standing.*

Paulette Nelson

CHAPTER 4: Family Trips - Keeping The Family Together

Family trips were always important to me, even as a child growing up my Dad would always make a family trip. We would travel to Tennessee to visit my Aunt, my Dad's sister or Washington to visit my Uncle. When we did our family trips, it was always a big deal. Once my children were of age to go we started taking our own family trips. We had wonderful friend's who would go with us, my husband's friends, as well as mines. I would always follow the children, even though they might have been embarrassed. If it was a senior trip, I was packing up the whole family and following the bus, Florida, Myrtle Beach and to the end of the world for my children. We would always have wonderful, fun, safe and blessed family trips.

We made some type of plans, even when my children had their own children we would try to have some time together, which is so important for families to try to stay together. God worships family, the devil tries to destroy families and God loves them. We have to remember that, it is amazing how the devil tries to come into your family and destroy it with things that tear you apart. I had to get ready for the empty nest syndrome. In 2009 my second oldest moved out of the home with my first granddaughter. I mean it was hard on me I had the pleasure of watching her grow from a newborn to the age of six. My daughter decided that she was grown, she was 28 years old, and she needed her own space. Her lifestyle was not what I thought it should be for her, so she decided hey, it is time, I have to make a move and stand on my own and she did it. She is still doing it, she is raising my oldest grandchild, and I am proud of both of them, I just pray God's strength for both of them. For all my children basically, and that they make decisions pleasing to God, that is my desire for all my children.

But family trips were very important, I think 2010 was the first year we didn't take a family trip, but praise God we still know that we love each other and that if there was anything that either one of us could do for each other we would.

CHAPTER 5: The Loss of My Father

My Father was an extra ordinary Christian man. He loved his wife, children, and grandchildren and looked forward to pleasing them. When I finally moved out years ago, we would talk all the time. My ex-husband would say, "My goodness you talk to your mom and dad like you haven't talked to them at all today." Nevertheless, that was our relationship, we would always keep up with each other, my Dad would go somewhere or I would go somewhere and would call each other. If my Mom were getting off at 2am, she would call and let me know she made it home, and I was away from the house.

I remember this funny story me and Dad would share, we would always talk about the basketball plays or what the ref was doing. We would talk about all kinds of things boxing, tennis, baseball or football. I recall my Mom saying, "I think I picked up the wrong child." She really thought she had picked up the wrong child, she never knew a girl child to be into sports as I was. My Dad and I loved all kinds of sports we would talk all the time especially once he retired we were able to talk about the Soaps. Every time we would come over he would have his housecoat on and he was in the bed. You could always tell when my Dad got dressed in a hurry, I would ask him to come over and start the fire for the grill or the kids needed to go somewhere. See my Dad wore these shoe-boots and you always knew he was rushing because he would have one pants leg rolled up stuck in the top of the boot and the other folded down correctly.

That was Deac! Awe he was just awesome, even when he did not feel well, he would just come and be there for me. If I needed a pipe fixed at the house or the water was leaking he was there, just anything to help me out, knowing that I was a single parent doing the best that I could and I truly miss him.

 However, getting back to always keeping in touch with each other, one time it was late! My mom was getting off work at 2am, and it was about 10pm the year was 1982 and my Dad was about 60 at the time. However, this one particular night I had called him around 10pm not sure of the reasoning, but he did not pick up the phone. I had told my husband that I could not reach him and that I was a little concerned. Probably an hour later I tried calling him again and the phone was busy, now I am thinking to myself, *'wow this is really strange.'* I ended up calling a neighbor of theirs that has known me since I was a kid and asked them had they seen my Dad? The neighbor had mentioned that his car was there, so now I am concerned so my husband and me packed the kids up and headed over to my parents house. Once we got there the neighbor who was about 70 at the time she came out with her gun and it was a little past midnight now, but we were going in there to see what was going on. Before we could step foot on the porch my dad comes pulling up with his friend, another Deacon from his church, and they had been hanging out. My Dad was so embarrassed, he likes, "What are you doing here?" He was just so embarrassed, this grown man being checked on because he did not check in! Nevertheless, he loved me for it; we laughed about that day all the time after it happened because that was just the type of relationship, we had. My children to this day continue to let me know where they are in some type of way. You know with this new technology, they can simply send a text and I appreciate anyway it is done!

In, 1996 I lost my Dad, and it amazes me how much you can still miss a person as if it were yesterday. I tell people all the time, *'I still miss him! I wish he was here to see all his beautiful grand/great grandchildren.'* He would just love them all! He would always spend time with them while he was here. Dad would always tell us not to yell at the grandchildren, because he was not a man to raise his voice for any reason in the world, my mom did all the yelling. I truly miss him, but I know when you lose someone it will either draw you closer to God or farther away. You have so many questions, how could God take the person that you really loved? Whether they were young or old, you loved that person and you wanted them to stay. However, knowing God helped me through it, because I know that he makes no mistakes and I will see him again, I will see my Dad again! That is one of the most special things about having a relationship with God; I do not understand how a person can make it through a loss without knowing God. Loss is like a sore, it heals but it still has a scab on it and sometimes I can just scratch on it and all these old memories and sadness come back to me, but I know I will see him again. So when you lose someone don't deny God, grow closer to him, when you stray that's when the devil get's in and tries to keep you from going to church, keep you from trusting God, don't do it! Rebuke Satan, ask God to help you understand that the loss is just temporary, and that with knowing God you will see them again. *This chapter was for my Dad, may God bless him and may he Rest In Peace! I may have been Broken Dad, But I am Still Standing.*

CHAPTER 6: Raising an Exceptional Child

Writing this chapter is a very difficult thing for me to do and once again, you cannot do it without God's help. Parents who are raising children with any type of special need I pray for your strength. I have had a child who is my only son! I knew that he was born into trauma through me. I had developed hypertension, high blood sugar, and I was unaware of my ex-husband's drug addiction at this critical time in my life. I was in the hospital 9 times trying to save the life of my unborn son, I had only gained 3 pounds during my term, I had placenta previa when he was finally born, and gallstones. I carried him the full 9 months; even with all the things that took place before and during the birth of my son, I knew he was totally a blessing and that God is going to have him come out on top.

He is now 24, but at an early age, he experienced a lot of difficulty and trauma. At the hospital when he was born, he developed a hernia; he was going back and forth to the hospital. He was around his father a lot when he was a baby and adored him, and then when he turned three his father was no longer in his life. My son had four women going through their own changes of life every month, with no male figure in his life. He was not adjusting to it very well, he had difficulty at school, and he could not stay focused. As a small child, he did not sleep at night, maybe 7 hours out of 24 for an entire year off and on. I remember the doctor asked me to document his sleeping pattern, and he would sleep 15 minutes here and there, he just never slept. I can recall taking him in for his 1 year well visit and they thought I was coming in to be checked, I looked that bad due to lack of sleep because my baby wouldn't rest.

However, God is good, I kept him in schools near my job because he had fear of going to school, and he would cry all the time. I had him tested when he was about five, and I guess ADHD was not prevalent in the late 80's, so they did not diagnose him with it then. I started him in therapy at the Children's Center because, he was having some issues with detachment, with me dating, and he was becoming self-destructive. The window shades were torn and he was completely acting out. I could not leave the house until I knew he was calm enough where he would not harm himself or others.

As he got older, he would not keep his room clean, he did not care about his hygiene, he was very emotional and high-strung. The teachers would call me on my cell phone to get him back in order, but I raised my kids not only to fear God but me as well, so when the teachers would call he would straighten right up. It takes a lot of patience, you cannot tell them a whole lot of things at one time because they are only going to pick out one thing. You have to try to keep them focus on one thing, at this time, you are going to clean your room or at this time, you are going to brush your teeth. It does not help to throw multiple things at your children. As a parent, you have to be very patient, calm, and direct. You have to remain very forceful, let them know who the boss is, do not show any fear, love them whole-heartedly and keep them in a close knit relationship with God.

There had come a time where they wanted to start treating him with medicine and I did not allow it at that time because I never wanted him to be in a twilight phase. As parents, there are decisions you have to make. Like whether or not to put your child on medications. He had wonderful teachers and counselors in his past, but the male teachers were the worse for him. They did not understand him because he was always the class clown, and it would always take the attention away from the class and the male teachers felt threatened by that. They could not keep the other students focused because they felt like my son had control over the classroom by gaining the attention of the others.

There is a very demanding type of support you have to offer children. Like my son, you have to remain supportive and keep counseling in the line, at one point I had later placed him on Paxil due to his emotional stress he faced about going to school and it did help him for a while, he was younger and I was able to get him to take his medicine. When he got older it got a little difficult for me, I was working more, not being able to spend time with him as I used to when he was younger. Sometimes they will get out of hand and he did, trying to get him to stay focused on staying in school. I remember he went to a community college praise God, and his sisters and me would tell him, *'when you graduate from high school we are going to throw you the biggest party.'* At that time, we did not think he was going to go that far because he just did not like school but he did and made it to a community college. Everyone was so excited for him and that is just an example of how awesome of a God we serve. We have to remember that with God, all things are possible and he did it, he graduated from high school! You have to put your trust in God and not in yourself, because you cannot do it alone. Believe me you cannot raise any child, especially one with a deficit or with challenges by yourself.

As a single mother, it was difficult, but we are coming along and we are making it. He attended a community college for a couple of years, made the Dean's List and ended up being accepted to a University. He never wanted to go away to school though. That was his biggest thing he did not want to leave home or his mother, but at times, you as the parent just feel like they have to get away. I made him go to a college, which was only 45 minutes away from home, and he came home every weekend, as the girls would do when they were away at school. He stayed at college for a year he did not do well there at all, so he came home.

My hopes are that in the future, institutions of higher education would acquire better knowledge, research, and support for children with ADHD. People with deficits need to feel safe and know that there are supporters that understand or are willing to help with whatever they may, be experiencing in the environment of higher education. I remember taking my son at an early age to Children's Hospital and going to the center where they helped disabled children. He would sit there with me and there would be children coming in with helmets, wheelchairs, and walkers and the parents would come over to me and ask me, "Well why is he here? Is he disabled?" Just because my son had no physical disabilities did not mean he did not need help, and I would tell them, "Yes he is, he has ADHD and he needs help as well." My son is very hand-some and that alone made the others angry or confused because he

Paulette Nelson

'looked normal.' ADHD was not acknowledged as a problem back then, because people could not see it visually externally, but my son was and is currently fighting a battle internally.

When he turned 14, he was finally diagnosed with ADHD and hyper-tension because he has had high blood pressure since he was 13. He had an eating disorder where he would just eat and eat. When he was away at school, he got the eating under control and lost a lot of weight, which in turn helped him with his blood pressure. Now at his current age of 24 he struggles to get a grasp on his emo-tions, outburst, and his anger. Anger seems to be a big thing, now that he's older, I think more demands are put on him as a 'Man' and being an 'African American Man' at that. There are so many expectations of men as a whole in society, which he just cannot keep up. He is struggling trying to keep a job, stay in school, remain out of the system, and on top of that, he has given me my fifth grandchild, so he is struggling to be a father to his daughter. Being a father is a lot of responsibility and sometimes it is just too much for these children.

As parents single or not we have to give them love, remain supportive, keep them focus, and give them structure. You have to watch their diet, keep them prayerful, and let them know that God is still there despite of all the things you may or may not be doing. The love and the emotional support is so important, parents I know it may seem hard! Trust me I know, I am not speaking from the side of my neck, I am speaking from experience that with God all things are possible. Our ADHD children need love also, so please find a support group, and if you have male children

Paulette Nelson

with no father present seek a male figure for them. If you have a daughter with ADHD then find some type of support for yourself that will help you support your daughter. My prayers are with you all and it can be done! We are expecting great things out of my son and they will happen with the support of his sisters and myself, may God bless my son, *Broken But Still Standing!*

CHAPTER 7: Life with My Grandchildren

My grandchildren are truly a blessing and a gift from God. I remember growing up and people would tell me, "Oh your kids are going to be very special, but your grandchildren are going to steal your heart." I would think to myself no, it is not possible for me to love anybody more then I love my four children, but they were right! They definitely have a special part in my heart.

My oldest and first granddaughter is the daughter to my second oldest, and she is seven now going on eight and she is such a joy. They lived with me until she was six, so she became a part of my life. She was mostly 'my baby', she is growing up very smart, intelligent, independent and she definitely gives my mom and me a lot of joy. We do not see her as often as we did when they lived here, so like I mentioned earlier I went through the 'empty nest syndrome', even with the grandchildren you go through that. I thank God for her and my daughter, who was younger when she had her, well she was 23 to be exact and she was a single mom as well. My daughter stayed in school, worked, and managed to complete her Bachelors degree while being a new mom. My granddaughter would come and visit with me on Saturdays and look forward to service on Sundays. My daughter has done a wonderful job in raising such an awesome little girl and I thank God for that!

My oldest daughter and her husband have blessed me with three grandchildren, my 1 and only grandson and two beautiful daughters. They are also very smart and they come over to visit once a week with me and my mom. My mom is bed-bound and she looks forward to seeing her great grandchildren when they come. They bring such joy to the house when they are all there. The children will get in the bed with her and watch movies or cartoons and my mom just adores them. They call me Nanny and my mom Granny, they are so smart, and everyone has a nickname. My daughter that still stays with me is Tee-Tee and my second oldest is Auntie and then of course Uncle. They are just some wonderful children!

My oldest daughter had retired at the age of 28 from being an Assistant Principal of an Elementary School; she has her Master's in Education. She decided to stay home and raise her children once she had her first child, with the support of her husband. She home schools her children who are doing exceptionally well with their studies. They are very smart, they love the Lord, very involved in church, and that is so important in raising children.

My son has given me my fifth and youngest granddaughter who is now 4 months and such a healthy little one already. They took her to the doctor last week and she weighed in at 13 pounds! My dad used to teach us as well as all his grandchildren how to blow 'spit bubbles' and I taught the baby how to do it and she picked it up like clockwork. The baby blows the bubbles all the time now, when we were kids it would drive my mother insane and it still does now. God is good, it is a blessing to have grandchildren, they do have a special part of my life, and I wanted to dedicate a little portion of this book to them. They are so important to me, they are my life and I want their parents to know that I am proud of all my children, and who they have all come to be *Broken, But Still Standing.*

My golden rule as it was so perfectly stated in Proverbs 22:6, *"Train up a child in the way he should go: and when he is old, he will not depart from it."* Therefore, you try to teach your children, so that when they have their children they will teach them in the same manner. Just remember no matter how old or young you are, keep God in the plan, keep your hand in God's hand and then you will not go wrong. Try to remember that you are a role model and an example not only for your children and for all the children that grace your presence. They see what you do and some try to emulate you and they also look up to

Paulette Nelson

you, because they need you. You as a parent have to sacrifice, that is all it is, and if you are not willing to sacrifice your life, your lifestyle, your joy, your sleep and sometimes your sanity then you should not have children. I used to tell my children when they were growing up, "I didn't ask to be here and neither did you so let's just make the best of it." We have to make the best of it and you have to be a team. When you have children spend time with them and put God first, love your children, teach them God's way and he will continue to help you. So many of us are left raising our grandchildren and I thank God that my children are still present and responsible enough to take care of their own children. However, if it happened to me I would still be able to help raise them with God's help. Therefore, stay strong parents and grandparents and consider it a gift from God when you are blessed with grandchildren, I do and I love them!

An Author's Note:

In these final two chapters, I am going to touch a little bit on relationships in my life with my mom, children, men in my life, and God. I will also talk about how it is to care for a parent. This is going to conclude the chapter as well as the book, and I can only hope that you have enjoyed it and that you gained some strength out of it.

CHAPTER 8: Parents Caring for Parents

My mom did not begin working until I was about fourteen, where she worked in the custodial department at a University. There she worked hard scrubbing floors and handling the day to day of a custodian. She was always a hard worker, she got there early and left late and the job was very well done. My mom has always been a person that did not mind helping people. She would give the neighbors money for mowing the lawn once they were not able to do it anymore. I remember the local drug abusers would ask if she needed anything and my mom would give them $10 for a burger. They would walk ten blocks to go get it that by the time they got back the sandwich would be cold. Keeping money has never been important to her! She always wanted to ensure that her family and siblings never wanted for much all the way down to the grandchildren, whatever she had she was willing to give it.

She was going to retire to help take care of my dad because he was sick by this time and her retirement date was going to be January 1, 1997, but he died in November of 1996. Therefore, she went on and retired and she was doing well going to church, cooking, and doing all the things she loved. In 1998, things started changing, she was not answering the phone, and she was giving more money than she should have to the drug abusers who would do errands for her. I would have to call the neighbors to see why she wasn't answering the phone, drive over at times and check on her, she started getting forgetful and couldn't remember important things, for example like when she drove she would get lost. Those things that were happening to her were the first signs of Dementia and Alzheimer's kicking in.

Towards the end of 1998, I was able to sell her house and I took my Florida room at my house, remodeled it, and made it into a bedroom for her, which is attached to mines. We moved her in and the doctor at the time had told me that eventually she will get to the point where she will not be able to walk and care for herself and you probably just need to put her in a nursing home. I got very offended from the statement the doctor made and switched physicians immediately. I was thinking to myself there is no way, I didn't put my dad in a nursing home and I've worked in a nursing home all my life and there is no way I'm going to put my mom in one. I guess I was in a better position with my children being home, all three of them were home except my oldest who was married and moved out. However, we all made an agreement even my oldest that we would take care of my mom, we are going to move her in and everyone is going to pitch in and help.

I was still working, so when she came she was able to walk into the house and then eventually she started having mini strokes and falling all the time. My mom went from walking, to a cane, then a walker, then a wheelchair and finally bed-bound. We get her up every day in a Geri- Chair, which is a unique chair created for people with similar situations, she is over 200lbs so she is quite heavy. I have had a dislocated shoulder, 2 discs in my back bulging but that is my mom and I am sure she would have done the same for me. Her mind is all over the place, at times she will think I'm her deceased sister, she doesn't eat like she used to, can't sit up in the chair long due to her C5 compression in her neck. Therefore, we try to get her out as much as possible to church and things like that so she will not be in the house all day and can remain oriented.

There has to be someone with her 24/7 so she cannot be left alone. Now that my second oldest and my granddaughter have moved out it is just my two youngest and me at home. My children are older now and have their own lives and I do not try to take that away from them because of my decision to take care of my Mom, they are supportive, but it is my mom. She often says to me, "God is the answer, No matter what the question" she is such a wonderful person. It gets harder to care for her because of the Dementia because she gets combative at times, but that is my mom and God gives me the strength despite of the things I am going through. I often go through the battle of one day I may have to put her in a nursing home, because my health is deteriorating and I'm getting older still trying to work and I can't do all the things I could have early on. It is hard, so for people who are caregivers I take my hat off to you, I take my hat off to those who have to care for a loved one, and I pray your strength. God gives us this strength; I know where I get the strength to just keep carrying on. He gives me the strength every day to get her up, bathe her, feed her, and change her. Just know that you are not alone if you made that decision to take care of a loved one. I have worked in nursing homes for years, and I have not found one yet that I feel comfortable with putting my mom in. I need to be assured that they would care for my mom as if she were theirs.

It is a hard task and I see how hard it is for people, I feel that people who are caring for the elderly and sick should have to pass a humanitarian class. A class that informs you if you have the kind of care and love in your heart to care for them despite of them cursing you out, trying to physically fight you, needing to be changed or just not feeling like being bothered. You have to have that patience and love for that person and your job. Just try to be strong and seek support from those you trust, take some time out for yourself, get help if you can. I am blessed to have family that will kick in and I know not everybody has that but you always have God. God will give you strength to endure, but if you have to make that decision to put them in a nursing home go and visit them and make it known that there are people there who love them. Make the facility aware that you are present and you know about the surveys and the correct type of care for your loved one. Do not take it for granted that they are being cared for, be there, let your loved one knows that you love and support them. That is my advice for people who have to leave their loved ones in the care of a nursing center just be there and make sure that the facility knows that you are present and aware. Know that God is with you and when you have done, all that you can do then you just have to stand and let God handle it. Ask him to help you make the right decisions. I thank God for my mom; she often calls us (my daughters and I) her angels. This is coming from a person who has loved us all our life. Parents are special, so care for them as much as you can and know that once they are gone, they are gone! There is no going back; when God calls them home there is nothing more you can do. So do what you can for your loved ones while you have them! God bless you all, I thank God for all the caregivers and all the parents caring for parents, remember God loves you and I do too, if you are broken its okay just remain standing!

CHAPTER 9: Relationships and Closing Stages

I am writing and dedicating this book to other women, to the struggle of a single parent, the struggle of a parent period. I am dedicating this book to a woman just trying to be a mother, a friend, a woman trying to be of God, a woman trying, to be a daughter; just a woman trying, that is torn from so many ways. Sometimes I feel like, we could just be cloned, that way we can be a mother and still be a daughter and still know who we are as an individual. We get lost in trying to maintain a job, raising children, being a wife, cooking, cleaning, maintaining a home, and taking care of your parents. We get lost in those things and we don't know who or where we are anymore, and as a woman who loves people, God, and loves to ensure that people are done right, sometimes I get very emotion-ally involved in how people are treated. That is so important to me!

I remember I had all four children and we were in line at a drug store, it was a long line and had many older people in the line. The people behind the counter were giggling and talking about what had happened the night before, my children at that time, were old enough to know their mother and what I believed in and that I would stand up for what I felt was right. I told my children to stay in line while I went to get a manager and I told him, "Listen you got older people in this long line with these cashiers back there talking about what they did last night, we are customers you need to get them in order." My children sometimes felt so embarrassed, but I will always stand up for what is right. When people are not treated, right I always felt like it was my job to say something. My mom is like that, very strong-headed, and an independent, woman that said what she felt. I know we as humans are suppose to remain *unbroken*. We have to be diplomatic about how we stand up for what is right. I myself am trying, remaining prayerful about that. Therefore, I will not be looked upon as a mean person, but as a person, who just wants people to be treated right and sometimes we lose that. I ask for everyone's prayers on that one. We as people, especially women, we have to stand up even when we are lonely we cannot just accept anybody in our life. I used to pray, and tell the kids to pray that no one who was not good or did not mean well by my family and me not be allowed into my life. I thank God that even with the relationships that I had they were with men who were family oriented and cared about my children and me. I had ended a previous relationship about 7 years prior with a man who just recently passed away. He was supportive and he helped me so much with the raising of my children because they were younger when we met. He would take them to school and pick them up, he helped me take care of my mom, God bless him, and may his soul rest in God's arms because he was a wonderful man. I am in a relationship now with a wonderful man, and I just want to say, sometimes we have to wait on the Lord and ask him to send someone in our life. Single parents you want someone who is going to be good to you and your children. I am still not married because I did not want anybody to come in and mistreat my children. You have to be prayerful and ask the Lord to order your steps. If you get lonely, for parents, get closer to your children and develop a stronger relationship with God. Do not just bring anybody into your life because you get lonely, ask the Lord to let you know who you are as a woman. Know that as strong, independent, and Christian women you can do all things with Christ.

Sometimes, children are selfish and they only think about themselves. I love my children and they love me and they all have different personalities, but we have to let them go and let God handle it. We have to let them go in their own direction and trust that God will bring them back. As a mother we just give too much of ourselves some-times, we sacrifice ourselves, We have to realize God is a jealous God, we have to give him some time, and our children time, our parents time but we have to give time to self as well. We have to know who we are even if it takes going to the movies, my mom used to say, "Even if you go buy yourself a pair of stockings, do something for you." Keep God first in your life, then your children, and your marriage, and learn how to balance them. Balance is a great word for women we have to learn how to balance. We are pulled in so many directions at times, taking the kids to school, going to work, and going to the grocery store, and other places. If it takes you writing out your tasks do that, do not overload your plate, and balance it instead!

Read your word, I try to read my daily word everyday and Lord knows I am far from perfect, but all I want to accomplish from my book is to help someone, just one person would be enough for me. I just want you to know you can do it and that you are not alone, God is there all you have to do is ask and it shall be given to you. We do not ask God, "What is it that you have for me, give me what you want."

That is my prayer now, God give me what you have for me, help me and show me what you have for me God. Ask and it shall be given, knock and the door shall be open, but you have to give God some time. Love yourself and know that you are here for a purpose and that you are a wonderful person. Have a good heart and share it along with love to the people around you, there are so many people who need it. So many children and older people need you. Therefore, you have to be able to stand sometimes, the pressure gets so hard and the devil will bring so much destruction and confusion your way, but you have to ask the Lord to rebuke satin. Do not allow these things to bring you down, we have to realize that we are not God and we cannot handle this by ourselves. The children, house being foreclosed, no money, and the things we consider trials and tribulations we cannot handle alone, we have to let go and let

Paulette Nelson

God handle it. Sure, it is very stressful, even for our African American men, but as soon as we do all that, we can do then we have to let it go. All that we go through and we are still standing, the health problems, mental issues, depression, not having enough money in our pockets.   All this is enough to tear a person down, but pick yourself back up, we all go or will go through it, just don't let it get you down, keep fighting.

This life is about fighting, not giving up, loving yourself, loving God, and knowing that you can do it. Just know that you can stand. Your heart may be broken, your health may have gotten you down, you may be in constant pain, and you may be so depressed because you lost someone you loved. You may have lost your house, you may have lost a job you were doing so well at, and you can't understand why they let you go, your friends may have abandoned you, but there is always a God right there asking for you to call on him. He has done it for me and I am no more special than you are and what he has done for me he will do for you! He loves all of us and we are his children and know that you are special and loved. I thank God for the special people in my life who know that I have made it only through Christ. The special people who were in my life who had loved my children and me I have a very special person now that is in my life. This man loves me for me and I thank God for him and I ask the Lord to bless him in a special way. God is good and I just want to thank him again for the people in my life who have seen me *Broken, But Still Standing!*

ABOUT THE AUTHOR

I am a child of God who loves the Lord. *"The Lord is my strength and my shield; my heart trusted in him, and I am helped..."* Psalm 28:7-9. My goal is to care and encouraged God's people through my life experience. I love people, the elders and children have a piece of my heart.

My children and I care for my mom. I have four children who I love dearly. I have five wonderful grandchildren. I am still employed. My vision is to stop working in a job setting and work in God's vineyard.

"And let us not be weary in well doing: for in due season we shall reap, if we faint not." Galatians 6:9

www.ingramcontent.com/pod-product-compliance
Lightning Source LLC
LaVergne TN
LVHW091207080426
835509LV00006B/879